99 Ways to
Influence Change

99 WAYS TO INFLUENCE CHANGE

Copyright © 2010 by Heather Stagl

ISBN: 978-0-557-76463-1

For information please write:
Enclaria LLC
12850 Hwy 9 N Suite 600-237
Alpharetta, GA 30004
www.enclaria.com

For Evan and Claire

*When something needs changing,
know that you can be the difference.*

Table of Contents

36. Prioritize

37. Give Praise

38. Educate

39. Help Them Succeed

40. Build New Skills

41. Do Favors

42. Fix Problems

43. Keep Promises

44. Remove Doubt

45. Laugh About It

46. Provide Useful Tools

47. Join Forces

48. Remove Dead Weight

49. Point to the Destination

50. Address Objections

51. Drop Names

52. Celebrate Success

53. Connect to Values

54. Say "Thank You"

55. Be Consistent

56. Extend an Invitation

57. Find the Emotion

58. Ask for Help

59. Incite a Riot

60. Identify Key Behaviors

61. Keep It Simple

62. Share What Works

63. Adjust the Environment

64. Hold Them Accountable

65. Induce Guilt

66. Respect Resistance

67. Go First

68. Gain Commitment

69. Make It Fun

70. Be Flexible

71. Measure Progress

72. Be Patient

73. Shrink It

74. Establish Authority

75. Get Leadership Support

76. Recognize Success

77. Generate Short-Term Wins

78. Eliminate Noise

79. Flatter

80. Empower

81. Nag

Introduction

There is no one size fits all solution. Every organization is different. And every change agent is unique.

Most books on influencing behavior distill their methodologies down to three to six steps. When it comes to organizational change, however, that is just too simple. Implementing change in a large group of people making up a complex structure takes a lot of different ways to get individuals to change their attitude, or try new things, or modify their behaviors.

If changing the behavior of others followed just a few simple steps, it would be easy! As someone who has tried to implement change in an organization, you know that it's usually not. In fact, it feels like pushing a giant boulder uphill. There are a lot of ways to influence people to change the way they work, and not all of them are effective in every situation or with every person.

This book is written for internal change agents: individuals, working from within organizations, who are trying to influence change from the middle. Like my clients at Enclaria LLC, change agents are found in roles like IT, organization development, human resources, process improvement, project management, strategic planning, sustainability, and any job in which you are responsible for changing the way people work without really having any authority to do so. All of the influence methods in this book are things you can do, even without having a leadership position.

When you set out to change your organization, or feel like everything you've tried hasn't worked to get people to budge, I hope you will turn to this book for inspiration. Most likely, you haven't tried all *99 Ways* in one situation! Nor would you want to.

Not all of the *99 Ways* are interchangeable. Some are personal influence strategies – those that are one-on-one, based on relationships; others are structural influence strategies – the systems, processes and tools you can create within an organization to cause or reinforce change. There are some you should use all the time, and several that you should only use sparingly or as a last resort. Some are instant, and some take more time to develop. Some you may already use without even knowing it. This list runs the gamut so you can become aware of the options available to you, and select methods that will work in your specific situation.

The list started as a compilation of the ideas in a number of books about influence and organizational change, which are noted in the resources section at the end of this book. It became a challenge to see how many different ways I could come up with to influence change. After I exhausted the books, I added more ways from my own experience and from the experience of my clients. Once I had the list, it needed explanation, so I started a daily blog. This book is the aggregation of those blog posts.

Although the influence strategies are numbered, they are not in any particular order. So, #1 is not inferred to be any more effective or important than #99. If you would like a free one-page checklist of all *99 Ways* so you can review them all at a glance, please visit:

www.enclaria.com/99-ways-to-influence-change

1. Tell Stories

Many times we try to convince people of the need for change using pretty graphs and clever slogans. If you want people to personally connect with what is going on, tell stories.

Consider the following narratives:
- Someone else with the same fears or concerns successfully made the change.
- A similar company didn't make the change and suffered the consequences.
- Another department succeeded in making the change, and this is how they did it.
- A senior leader did something out of the ordinary that shows unwavering commitment to the change.

Telling stories helps people relate to change so they can imagine themselves doing it. Stories also reinforce the graphs and slogans with real-life examples, so they can believe that change can happen. So, collect, create and tell stories to influence change.

2. Model Behavior

"Example is not the main thing in influencing others; it is the only thing." ~Albert Schweitzer

While I obviously believe there are at least 98 other ways to influence others, he has a point; if you want people to change their behavior, you have to do it too.

Modeling behavior influences in three ways. First, you show "the right way" so people learn how to do it. Second, you demonstrate commitment by being willing to do it yourself.

The third way that modeling behavior influences is rooted in psychology. Studies show that the power of conformity – the compulsion of humans to go along with group behavior – is significantly reduced when at least one other person is going against the group. When you choose to become that person by performing the new desired behavior, then you help others see that it is okay to do something different from the norm. They will often join you.

In order for modeling behavior to work, people have to be watching. If you are not in the position to set an example, find someone who is and make sure she models it as well.

3. Involve People

I often hear (or read) the phrase, "People don't resist change; they resist being changed."

No one wants change to be imposed on them to the point of helplessness and lack of control. If you try to force it, you are headed for a full-on revolt.

Instead, involve people in shaping the change, so it doesn't feel like it is happening *to* them, but *with* them.

- Ask them to help develop the new process that they will be using in their jobs.
- Involve them in decisions that will affect them.
- Invite them to design the report or the tool or the form they will use every day.
- Find out what else they think should be fixed during the implementation.

Not only will you reduce resistance by giving people some control over their own situation, but the end result will be better because you involved them.

4. Say "Please"

Never underestimate what people will do if you just ask nicely!

First of all, you have to ask. Forget all the complicated programs, messages and incentives for a minute. What would happen if you simply asked people to take part in the new activity, or to adjust their behavior? Sometimes we think we need to add all the fancy stuff when really all we need to do is ask the question.

Also, remember your manners. *Please* remember your manners. "Please" removes the demanding attitude, and replaces it with respect. One word changes a statement from an expectation to a personal request. Adding "please" with emphasis may also increase the sense of urgency.

Say "please." (*Please.*) It is the magic word, after all. Couldn't your change initiative use a little magic?

5. Allow Failure

When trying out a new activity, process or behavior, not everyone – in fact few people – will get it right the first time. And that is okay. It must be okay. Better than that, it must be encouraged.

Much of resistance to change comes from:
- Fear of failure
- Feeling incompetent
- Fear of screwing something up
- Not wanting to be judged
- Fear of being wrong
- Fear of looking dumb.

All that anxiety makes some people avoid trying and learning something new. First, equip people appropriately so they feel confident to try. Then let them know it is okay and even expected for them to mess up the first few (or 20) times. Ask them how you can best handle it when they do. And, do what you can to ensure people do not encounter ridicule, frustration, impatience or disdain from others when they do something wrong. Otherwise, they may not try again.

6. Ridicule

Some of the influence tactics in this book should be used sparingly and with caution. But in some situations, they can be effective! We often use them without even thinking about it. One of those is ridicule.

Pay attention to the next time you use sarcasm or jokingly make fun of someone to get them to do what you want him to do. Most likely, it will be with a friend or someone else you feel comfortable being irreverent around. You may not want to admit it, but you do it because it works.

You should only taunt someone whom you know well, and always in good humor. The last thing you want to do is hurt someone's feelings or offend him by striking a nerve, so ridicule coworkers with caution. But, insinuating that your colleague doesn't want to try something because he is a wimp, or is not smart enough, or whatever he would want to prove wrong might spring him into action.

Sure, ridicule is not going to make it on the list of most ethical influence tactics. If you ridicule excessively, you will be viewed as a bully or a clown. But occasional friendly teasing is also one way to nudge someone or to correct behavior.

7. Generate Scarcity

Part of the challenge of influencing change is getting people to step out of their day-to-day routines to take some action, instead of saying, "I'll just do it later."

One way to encourage people to take action now is to generate scarcity. When people perceive that an opportunity is scarce, it creates demand for that opportunity.

Usually you see this influence tactic in sales campaigns, like "limited time only" offers and early bird discounts. The same principle can be used to create demand for your change initiative. Consider the following examples (the numbers are arbitrary):

- Limit volunteer opportunities, like teams or training, to 8 people.
- Encourage people to show up to meetings on time by having 2 fewer chairs than attendees.
- Set an end date for award eligibility.
- Offer recognition or privileges to the first 5 people who take the desired action.

Be creative! Find a way to generate scarcity and create demand for change.

8. Transfer Ownership

For each initiative, the change agent should be a temporary position. Eventually, ownership of the new organization, process or system must be turned over to the people who are doing the work.

I'm not talking about giving people a sense of ownership by involving them. I mean giving the job back to them to take care of from now on.

Ownership means they are personally responsible and accountable for conducting business the new way. Their independence from you as a change agent is the only way to know that the initiative was successful.

Of course, you can transfer ownership of smaller pieces of the initiative before the change is complete. Perhaps certain reports, meetings, processes or tasks are ready to be handed over. Let them have it!

One of my clients led a team that had not been completing its tasks. Since it was a lower priority than some of her larger projects, she felt she didn't have time to follow up or take on the tasks herself. She decided to delegate team leadership to another member of the team. After just one e-mail inviting her to take over and giving her direction, the new team leader took it and ran with it. Now the team is moving forward, and my client only needs to check in occasionally. She is spending less time on that program, the team is thriving, and change is happening - because she let go.

Once you transfer ownership, true installation of the change has begun.

9. Clarify Expectations

Based on many years of research, Gallup, Inc. has developed 12 statements that best predict employee engagement and performance (called the Gallup Q12®). One of those statements is, "I know what is expected of me at work."

It's obvious, really. If you have expectations for what people should do as they go through the change, then tell people what they are, so they can try to meet them! Especially in times of uncertainty and change, people don't want to guess what you really want them to do.

Expectations take the form of results, behaviors, or attitudes. Results are what you want them to accomplish. Behaviors are what you want people to do, or the manner in which you want them to accomplish the results. Attitudes are the way they feel toward the change and how they express themselves about it.

Clarifying expectations can also be a collaborative effort. When you share your personal expectations with people, find out if they think they can meet them. Then negotiate to realistic shared expectations, instead of expecting the impossible without their input. You can also ask for their expectations of you.

10. Provide Feedback

As people incorporate changes into their routines, let them know what they are doing well and what needs improvement as they go. Feedback provides reinforcement of the change and also the opportunity for course correction.

When we hear the word "feedback," we typically think of difficult one-on-one conversations telling people their "opportunities for improvement." While that is one form of feedback, consider these other ways to let people know how they are doing:

- Audio or visual cues indicating a task has been performed correctly or incorrectly
- Data, charts, test results or other information that indicate progress
- Employee surveys or other anonymous feedback tools.

The people who need the most feedback during change are leaders. Since it is typically daunting to provide leaders with feedback, they are also least likely to actually receive feedback. In your role as a change agent, it is imperative to find a way to tell leaders what they are doing to hinder the change effort, and not to forget to let them know what they are doing right. If you don't tell them, how else will they know?

11. Establish Urgency

In his book *Leading Change*, John Kotter listed "Establish a sense of urgency" as step #1 of 8 on the path to change. Daryl Conner introduced the metaphor of the burning platform in *Managing at the Speed of Change*.

Both classic change management books agree; if you want people to move somewhere else, you need to make their current position incredibly uncomfortable. Make it unfathomable to choose to stay where they are. Let them know the status quo is not sustainable. Give people a reason to change.

In my *Change Starts Here* workbook, the first step on the path to change is to clarify the current reality of the organization and the change you want to implement. If you want to create a map to get somewhere else, you need to start by figuring out where you are — and determine what you need to move away from. Help others understand the danger of staying on the current path so they can feel the need to change.

12. Remove Enablers

In 1519, Spanish conquistador Hernán Cortés, upon arrival to what is now Mexico, ordered his men to scuttle the boats so they could not leave. (Legend says he burned them, although history shows they merely ran the boats ashore.)

Until the change has been firmly established, the temptation remains to go back to the old way. It is safe and reliable. The new way has yet to be proven.

For example, one key to staying on a diet is to throw all the bad-for-you food out of your pantry and not replace it when you go to the grocery store. That way, it is not available when you want a snack. You would have to choose a healthier option or not eat anything at all.

Similarly, one way to force change is to eliminate the option to return to the old way. Remove the previous software. Delete the old spreadsheet. Throw away the old templates and forms. Remove the status quo enablers. Burn the boats.

13. Acknowledge Fear

One of the key elements of resistance to change is fear. Fear can keep people from trying new things, stop people from speaking up during their change experience, and create anxiety about the future.

Most changes that are intended to create high-performance organizations have some element of reducing fear involved. Whether you want to increase employee engagement, improve teamwork or encourage people to take more risks, employees will have to deal with willingness to trust, uncertainty, and the common fears of failure, being wrong or looking foolish.

In the book *Driving Fear Out of the Workplace*, authors Kathleen Ryan and Daniel Oestreich state that the first step to reducing fear is to acknowledge its presence. Essentially, you can't deal with something until you recognize that it exists. Let people know that fear is natural and expected during change, so they can help you illuminate it and understand it. When the source of fear is identified, usually people see that it is really not so scary after all.

14. Show You Care

The best way I know to gain respect as a change agent is to show that you care about people personally. People are more likely to go along with you, even in difficult times, if they feel you have their best interests at heart.

Of course it starts with actually caring – a good dose of empathy is always good. I don't recommend pretending to care when you really don't. People can sense insincerity, especially since they will be watching for it during times of change.

So, get to know people personally. Understand how the change is affecting them. Advocate on their behalf for what they need during the change. Show that you genuinely care about them as fellow human beings.

15. Start Conversations

Confusion and hesitancy about change occurs when the only conversations about change happen around the water cooler, or behind closed doors, or as whispers in the hall. Even with clear official communication, without open conversations people can form their own interpretation of what is going on.

The most important conversations are usually the ones people would rather avoid. Create safe environments so people can talk about concerns, share ideas, and productively process the change, either one-on-one or in groups. Provide the opportunity to discuss the otherwise undiscussable with someone who can do something about it.

As an individual, it is probably impossible for you to have conversations with everyone in the organization who is impacted by the change. It is important to equip managers and supervisors with the information and skills they need to have conversations about the change with their direct reports. That way, you get the whole organization talking about the change in an open, constructive manner.

16. Demand Compliance

Sometimes, if you want people to do something, you've got to use brute force. Enough with the buy-in and consensus-building efforts; just make people do it already!

I've known plenty of change agents who tried to implement new processes whose efforts were foiled by a boss who did not demand compliance to that process. If you wait for everyone to use the new process because they want to, you might be waiting a long time. At some point, someone might have to say "this is the way we're going to do things" and then not accept any alternatives.

One of my clients struggled with the idea of demanding compliance without being a jerk. He had a dominant personality already, and didn't want to rely on being an authoritarian leader. We decided that demanding compliance is about making decisions with input from the team, and then sticking to those decisions even when people complain or make excuses. It is not about controlling or ignoring the concerns of others. It is a resolve to not be wishy-washy about change.

Of course, to have any effect, demanding compliance requires that you have some authority to insist that people tow the line. Otherwise you are just a bossy windbag who will probably be ignored.

17. Develop Support Systems

Many familiar programs designed to help individuals form better habits surround people with support systems. For instance, according to WeightWatchers®, "People who attend meetings lose 3 times more weight as those who go it alone." Their website says that meetings provide guidance, encouragement and accountability for those who attend.

If support systems work for changing personal habits, why not for organizational change? I once formed a peer group of cross-functional directors that met for lunch on Fridays to improve our leadership skills. We discussed leadership articles and conducted an internal 360 degree feedback questionnaire (although only being peers and self I suppose it was only 180 degrees). Not only did we have eye-opening discoveries about our personal leadership traits, but the group also improved cohesiveness.

Support systems might also take other forms: A website to look up the answers to questions. A phone number to call when someone is stuck. A trusted name to reach out to when someone has a question or needs some help. Provide people with a means of knowing that they don't have to go through change alone.

18. Admit Mistakes

Mistakes happen during the course of organizational change: lack of communication, bad strategy, poorly aligned incentives, misdiagnosing of a problem, and other leadership bobbles. It can be tempting to smooth them over, make a course correction and hope nobody noticed. Or worse yet, let the change initiative fizzle out and disappear without explanation.

The trouble is, every day people give you permission as a change agent to mess with their jobs, their routines and their habits. They give you their time and attention to learn and try something new. And that is a privilege that must be earned.

If a mistake has been made that requires altering course, admit the mistake. Let people know what happened, what the new path is and how you plan to avoid similar mistakes in the future. Perhaps an apology is appropriate. Otherwise you wear down their resilience and their trust in you. Cynicism about change – and increased resistance to future changes – can occur when mistakes go unacknowledged by those who made them.

19. Make It Viral

In today's attention-overload workplace, it is easy for your change message to be lost. With the advent of social media sites like Twitter, Facebook and YouTube, it seems the only way to gain a lot of attention nowadays is to make your message viral. That is, it needs to gain momentum by spreading from person to person.

First, make the message or activity something that people will want to share with friends and coworkers – for example: entertaining, informative, fascinating, fun or helpful. Next, build in the capability for people to share what they learn or what they are doing, perhaps add the ability to rate it or comment on it. Some examples:

- A quiz about the organization's strategy in which employees can challenge each other to beat their high score
- A volunteer activity sign up form where employees can invite their coworkers to participate
- An idea contest in which employees encourage their colleagues to vote for their ideas

Of course, enabling a change message to go viral requires letting go of control, but in exchange it becomes more visible and can gain momentum on its own. And if it doesn't have the intended effect, you will be able see that easily as well.

20. Remove Obstacles

Often, some people in the organization are on board with the change, but too much stands in their way! Even if they want to, they may not modify their activities and behaviors because they are unable or uncomfortable doing so. To enable change, you need to remove obstacles.

As part of a strategic initiative to increase innovation, I once conducted a survey to understand what kept people from sharing ideas. It wasn't that they didn't see opportunities or didn't want to help the company succeed! Instead, the survey showed a number of barriers that prevented people from wanting to speak up.

Consider the following potential obstacles to change:
- Not enough time to add a new activity to their routine or to move through the learning curve
- Outdated rules, policies and procedures
- Insufficient equipment, tools or software
- Lack of support from managers.

Help employees who are advocating for the change to identify the barriers to change. Then, work to get these obstacles out of the way!

21. Show Others Are Doing It

Under ambiguous circumstances, we look around to see what other people are doing to help us understand the situation and select the appropriate action ourselves. Robert Cialdini, author of *Influence: The Psychology of Persuasion*, calls this phenomenon "Social Proof" and says it is rooted in conformity. If you want to influence someone to do something, show that others are already doing it.

How does this work in organizational change? Here are some examples:

- Showcase early adopters so people can see that "real" employees (not just change agents) are using a new system or process.
- Coach key people prior to meetings to demonstrate new behaviors.
- Recruit people to be the first to sign up on a volunteer list.
- Report the number or percentage of people who have participated in the change (i.e. accessed an online system, completed a survey, or went through training).

The power of Social Proof and conformity is strong. To feel it in action, just get on an elevator and try to face away from the door. Even in an empty elevator it seems awkward! You can harness this same phenomenon to influence change in your organization. Just find ways to show that others are doing it.

22. Tell the Truth

If change starts anywhere, it starts with the truth. Someone sees the organization as it is and how it could be better, and then starts talking about it with anyone who will listen.

It doesn't help to keep a little blue notebook full of observations, complaints and ideas. Change won't start until you do something about it – which usually means speaking up.

That does not mean that you should complain or talk behind someone's back, even if it's the truth! Doing so will only serve to destroy your credibility. If you want your words to result in change, it only works to tell the truth constructively to someone who can do something about it.

Even after the change starts, the truth still needs to be told. New aspects of culture will be uncovered. People will need honest feedback and accountability. Teams will need a facilitator who can speak the things that others will stay silent about.

If you want to affect change in your organization and truly take on the role of the change agent, you need the courage to tell the truth.

23. Ask For Ideas

Want to know what needs changing in your organization? Just ask the people who work there.

It's amazing how people spout long-held ideas for improvement that are unleashed when someone simply asks for them. With great enthusiasm, employees will share what they have long known was a problem but no one seemed to want to know about it. Dig past the complaints, and often you will find that people also have thought of a solution.

In order to create a safe environment for sharing ideas, defer judgment. Provide some direction to focus creativity. Help people improve on their ideas so they can be acted upon. Follow up, report progress, and implement. Show employees that their ideas matter, and they will keep providing more.

When you have a groundswell of people in the organization thinking about opportunities for change, you create an atmosphere of possibility. There is a big difference in mindset between *Not*-Invented-Here and Invented-Here!

24. Make It Easy

Consider the following scenarios:

1. As a team facilitator, you diligently take notes, capturing all the tasks, responsibilities and due dates for the team. After the meeting, you send out an email to the entire distribution list with the notes as an attached document.
2. As a team facilitator, you diligently take notes, capturing all the tasks, responsibilities and due dates for the team. After the meeting, you take a few minutes to sort out each team member's tasks and send them out separately to each individual in the body of an e-mail marked "Your responsibilities for next week's meeting."

Which team would you expect to complete more of the tasks for next week? The one where the team facilitator made it easy to see what needs to be done. Specific expectations. No extra clicks. No digging to find what to do.

So often, we design change so people need to jump through hoops in order to accomplish it. Think about the effort you expect people to expend, and see what you might eliminate or reduce (albeit with some extra effort on your part). The easier you make change for the people going through it, the easier change will be.

25. Rely on Friends

Your closest circle of influence are your friends at work. They are the people who trust you the most, who like you, and who believe in what you are doing – at least they see that you believe in it. Perhaps with the exception of people who report directly to you, you have the greatest influence with your friends at work.

Being a change agent is a difficult job to do alone. Rely on your friends to help you! The following are three roles your friends can play in the changes you spearhead:

- Cheerleader: Need encouragement? Friends are good for that.
- Sounding board: Need some quick feedback? Ask a friend what he thinks.
- Guinea pig: Need someone to be the first to try the new procedure, software, meeting format, etc.? Experiment on your friends!

I'm not suggesting that you take advantage of your friends without reciprocity. As in any relationship, relying on your friends to help you implement change is a two-way street. Always be there when your friends need your expertise and help in return.

26. Beg

Desperate times call for desperate measures. And what is more desperate than begging?

Although getting on your knees and crying will most likely not win you favor with coworkers and managers, a little begging might work to show someone that you really need her to do something.

Begging can be subtle, like going the more playful route of "Please... Pretty please... Pretty please with sugar on top..." Or, it can be more urgent and imploring, like, "I beg of you, please stop saying that!"

It is important for your dignity that you escalate your request with increasing urgency without sounding desperate; that assumes, of course, that maintaining your dignity is more important than getting the point across. For the sake of your reputation and relationships, use this method of influence sparingly.

27. Instigate Competition

Want to motivate people to reach for a goal? Tap into the human drive to win, and instigate competition. Whether there is an award or not, individuals and teams will most likely strive to earn bragging rights over the rest of their competitors.

Several years ago, I worked for a company that held a contest to encourage idea generation. They offered large dollar prizes for the top three ideas (first place was $5,000), as judged by the executive committee. The competition generated a large number of ideas submitted to the contest, which resulted in many improvements for the company. Of course, after the contest was over, the number of ideas dried up.

Beware; when you instigate competition, you can turn teammates into enemies. You may further entrench silos in the organization if those silos are competing against each other. If you want to encourage collaboration between individuals or groups, don't instigate a competition between them. Instead, put them on the same team against another foe (like the real competition in the marketplace!).

28. Instill Curiosity

One client organization launched a successful communication campaign for its strategy with posters that simply said, "Got strategy?" The posters, which had white printed on a black background and were printed with the same font as the "Got milk" ad campaign, also included a date — that of the next round of communication, when people would find out what the strategy was, and why it was important to know. The change agents at that organization relied on the premise that if you want people to pay attention, instill curiosity.

It's the curious who follow clues and seek out answers, whether they wonder what a poster is talking about or they want to find out if there is a solution to a problem. If curiosity killed the cat, it was because the cat was actively trying to satisfy that curiosity, and not resting lazily in the sun as a cat would otherwise do.

Entice people to wonder about the change initiative by adding an element of mystery. Give them a question to ponder so they are waiting for an answer. Or, you may even require that they do some work themselves to figure out the answer, to increase participation. Present a puzzle, and benefit from the sense of curiosity each of us has to solve it.

29. Reframe It

People going through change often get stuck in their current state because their existing point of view keeps them from seeing other possibilities for moving forward. The stories they tell themselves about their experience of the change can reinforce their resistance. When someone is stuck in his point of view, reframe it.

Reframing means helping people see things from new perspectives. The following steps outline the general process of reframing:

1. Acknowledge that they are stuck.
2. Understand their current point of view.
3. Offer alternative viewpoints.
4. Explore what might be true, useful and important about the alternative viewpoints.
5. Help them to choose the best perspective for moving forward.

For example, someone might feel like the change is happening to him, like he is being changed. His current perspective is that he has no control over what is happening to him. You might reframe his perspective by exploring what he does have control over, or by suggesting ways he might get more involved and have a say in what is happening to him. Help others change perspectives, and you will change minds.

30. Facilitate Meetings

With as many hours as we spend in meetings, they are definitely the bane of corporate life. While meetings are the default method of getting people together to solve problems and make decisions, often they are a waste of time for the attendees instead.

As a change agent, meetings are a key tool you can use to drive your change initiative forward. However, productive meetings don't happen just because people sit in a room together. You must deliberately facilitate meetings to make them effective.

Some of the many responsibilities of a meeting facilitator are:
- Get the right people in the room
- Determine intended outcomes
- Stay on topic
- Guard ideas
- Coach for effective team dynamics
- Ensure accountability
- Make it fun.

One way to increase support for your change initiative is to not make people dread getting together to talk about it. When you facilitate meetings, they will start to be meaningful and productive, and even enjoyable.

31. Set the Default

In their book, *Nudge: Improving Decisions about Health, Wealth, and Happiness*, authors Richard Thaler and Cass Sunstein talk about how people are likely to continue a course of action simply because it is the one they are already doing. This status quo bias is not a surprise to anyone trying to influence organizational change! However, when designing change initiatives, we can tap into this phenomenon by setting the default to the behavior we want to see.

For example, is the change something that people need to opt into or opt out of? If the default is that people do not participate and need to sign up (opt in), then research shows that fewer people will participate than when the default is that people are signed up and need to take action to not participate (opt out). People will generally stick with the automatic status they are given.

How might this look in organizational change?
- Scheduling people to attend meetings or training sessions about the change
- Including every department in the report measuring participation
- Automatically enrolling new employees in the program
- Setting system defaults on the company intranet or other software.

When designing your change initiative, consider what the unstated default might be. Then, assess whether that default is the new status quo you would like to create. Set the default to the automatic decision you would like people to make.

32. Build Trust

To have any influence at all as an individual, other people need to give you the power to influence them. And no one willingly gives power to someone he doesn't trust. To build a foundation of trust, start by protecting your integrity. In a great book called *The Transparency Edge*, Barbara Pagano and Elizabeth Pagano offer nine ways to build credibility and integrity:

- Be completely honest.
- Gather intelligence. (Get feedback.)
- Compose yourself.
- Let your guard down.
- Keep your promises.
- Deliver bad news compassionately.
- Say you're sorry.
- Watch your mouth. (e.g. Don't talk behind other people's backs.)
- Applaud freely and regularly.

As a change agent, you also need to build trust in the change itself, which means building trust in the leaders who are driving it. People going through change need to be confident that leaders are capable of delivering it. The leaders themselves also need to be trustworthy. Help them protect their integrity by providing feedback when necessary, so they have the opportunity to correct any behaviors that reduce trust.

33. Listen

Sometimes people resist or resent change because they feel they have no control of their situation. Often this feeling of lack of control stems from not having an outlet for their frustration or their ideas. As a change agent, you can mitigate some resistance simply by listening.

Listening goes beyond just letting someone flap her lips with you in the vicinity. In the book *Co-Active Coaching*, the authors describe three levels of listening:

1. Internal listening: The focus is on the spoken words and their meaning to you (as the listener).
2. Focused listening: Your attention is on the other person. You notice not only what she says, but how she says it and what she doesn't say. You focus on the meaning to her. Level 2 listening is where understanding, collaboration, empathy, and clarification happen.
3. Global listening: You bring more of your intuition to the listening, feeling the energy and changes to the environment.

At Level 1, most people will not feel as though you are truly listening to them. To show that you understand requests and concerns, your best listening as a change agent will happen at Level 2. Even if you are unable to fulfill requests and fix concerns, if you are fully listening to people going through change, they will feel that their opinions and experiences count.

34. Bribe

While it sounds illicit, bribery is simply offering something in exchange for what you would like another person to do. Mutual back-scratching or trading favors are common ways to influence someone who doesn't believe the value of performing an activity is worth the effort to do it. A little extra incentive might push some people over the hill of resistance.

Note: I am not suggesting that you offer or request anything illegal or unethical! Perhaps you might offer to take someone out to lunch if he will do something to help move change forward. Or you might put in a good word with management. Or trade vacation weeks. Or use your influence on his behalf.

The trouble with bribery (besides riding the margin of ethics) is that it can become an expectation. Like offering candy to a child to be quiet, you might find that the person will want future favors in exchange for continuing his "proper" behavior. Use with extreme caution!

35. Encourage

Change can be intimidating for those going through it. Taking on new behaviors, especially those that conflict with the existing culture of the organization, require people to do things that are uncomfortable. As a change agent, you can help by encouraging.

Literally, "to impart courage," there are many ways you can encourage others: Reassuring them that it will be ok. Reminding them that they are qualified and capable. Telling them they will be better for it. Walking them through a tough scenario. Or letting them know you support them and will help them deal with what comes next.

The opposite of encouragement is abandonment. Leaving people to provide all of their own personal motivation also means they have to fight off the negative voices in their heads on their own as well. It's important to show people that you believe they can make the required changes, to help them believe it of themselves.

Sometimes people going through change need a little nudge forward. Instill confidence, and encourage others to take that next step.

36. Prioritize

In most cases the day-to-day activities, meetings, and tasks continue at the same time as change is taking place. It is easy for change to be a peripheral activity, something to fit between everything else, or something to complete when everything else is done. To influence change, help people prioritize.

Prioritizing is not just about helping people understand the urgency and importance of change. How does its importance stack up against everything else? It doesn't work for the change initiative to be relegated to people's free time, nor does it work for everyone to stop running the company so they can focus only on the change. What can slide, and what is more important than the change?

Unless people already had excess capacity, either the capacity needs to increase to absorb the work of change (either by adding people or adding hours), or the amount of work needs to be adjusted to fit the capacity. As a change agent, work with employees and managers to prioritize activities so the change can be done effectively and also given its due importance.

37. Give Praise

My dog Sadie, a Boston Terrier, is now 9 years old, but I remember
when we brought her home as a puppy. The first thing on the list?
House-training. I had heard that the best book on dog training is *How
to Be Your Dog's Best Friend* by the Monks of New Skete. Their advice
is simple. Take the dog out in regular intervals. When they go in the
right spot, you praise them: hoot, holler, cheer, smile, clap! Good girl!
If they have an accident, you admonish the dog with a growl, take them
outside and show them where to go. When they go there, praise them
again!

Lo and behold, years later when we potty-trained our son (and are
now going through it with our daughter), the book *Toilet Training in
Less Than a Day* by Nathan H. Azrin recommends essentially the same
course of action! And it worked just as effectively.

Am I comparing working adults to puppies and toddlers? Yes!
Because we all enjoy receiving praise, no matter what age and maturity.
We want reassurance and recognition that we are doing a good job.
And, the good news for change agents is that giving someone praise for
doing something correctly reinforces the behavior and improves the
likelihood that he will do it again!

Be generous with praise. It is free and incredibly effective.

38. Educate

When change is happening to people without sufficient explanation, they will instinctively resist it. To help people understand what is going on, it is important to let them know what the change is and why it is happening. To influence change, educate people about the change itself.

Answer the natural questions people will want to know to help them decide to get on board:

- What is the change?
- Why are we doing it?
- What are the goals?
- What's in it for me?
- How will I be affected?
- What is required for this to be successful?
- When will it start and end?
- Who is supporting this?

Use multiple communication vehicles to inform people about the change. Typical top-down vehicles include newsletters, town hall meetings and e-mail blasts. Also, make sure education about the change occurs in one-on-one conversations and team meetings between managers and employees to make it personal.

39. Help Them Succeed

For two years in a row, one of my fellow colleagues at a local learning community for organization change professionals has provided feedback as I designed exercises for the presentations I gave to the group. Both times, he asked a remarkable question: "How can you help people succeed?"

Whenever it is possible for someone to make an error, someone will. Wherever there is an opportunity for confusion, someone will be confused. Wherever someone can get stuck, someone will get stuck. And, anyone who is confused or makes an error or gets stuck will naturally become frustrated and disillusioned with the task at hand.

What helps people succeed depends on the activity. In the case of my presentations, helping the audience succeed meant providing instructions, an example, a template, and ample time to complete the exercises. Many years ago, when I worked on the implementation team of an enterprise-wide IT system, helping users succeed included providing reports and one-on-one, on-the-job training for each person.

As you design the change initiative, consider that no one else in the organization is as familiar with it as you are. It is easy to make assumptions that people will know what to do without detailed instructions or examples. Take a step back and determine where people might need a little extra help to succeed.

40. Build New Skills

In order to change, people need both the desire and the ability. Change often requires that people learn how to perform new tasks and behaviors, so they have the ability to participate effectively in the change. For your change to be successful, you may need to build new skills in the people going through the change.

New skills vary by change initiative, but they might include:
- Time management
- Creativity
- Team facilitation
- Leadership
- Measurement and analysis
- Computer skills.

Prepare people for the change by providing the skills they need to perform well in the new organization. Identify the new behaviors, tasks and activities that are required to implement change. Ensure that the people you expect to do them have the skills to participate successfully.

41. Do Favors

In *Influence: The Psychology of Persuasion*, author Robert Cialdini talks about the principle of reciprocity: people tend to return a favor. Do something nice for someone, and he is likely to do something nice for you in return. As a change agent, your personal influence with individuals can be enhanced by this principle. To influence change, do favors for people.

Saying that you should do lots of favors so people will owe you favors in the future sounds manipulative, I realize. No one with integrity wants to think of purposely doing good deeds with the intent to rack up points that you can cash in later. But it's a simple psychological principle. We have more influence with people who like us, and one way to get people to like you is to do favors for them.

I don't recommend only doing favors for people whom you would like to gain influence; generally we call people who do that brown-nosers! Instead, do favors for everyone. Be generous with your time, knowledge, expertise and power, because as a change agent you never know who you will need to influence. Do favors because it's the right thing to do, and trust that your personal influence will grow.

42. Fix Problems

Want people in your organization to get on board with your change initiative? Show them how the change will fix an existing problem! Give them a solution (or better yet, work with them to develop a solution) to a nagging issue, and they will thank you for your help.

In my experience, people will gladly put in the effort to make their jobs easier, more effective or more meaningful. Help them fix something they've been complaining about, and you will get raving fans.

Early in my career, as an industrial engineer, I frequently redesigned labor-intensive manufacturing processes. At first, I tried designing the systems from a purely engineering point of view, but I quickly found that is not a good way to get workers on board! Instead, it was much more effective to first understand the existing problems that workers experienced, and then integrate the solutions as part of the design and communication of the new process.

As your project progresses, scope creep will naturally happen as related problems can also be solved within the context of the project. As long as the budget and time line can support it, go ahead and expand the scope! Fixing additional problems will go a long way toward gaining the support of people whose jobs will be better for it.

43. Keep Promises

Earning the ability to influence people in your organization requires that you maintain your integrity. One simple way to demonstrate your trustworthiness and credibility is to keep your promises.

Keeping promises goes beyond the literal promise. According to the authors of *The Transparency Edge: How Credibility Can Make or Break You in Business*, the following are also examples of keeping promises:

- Uphold commitments
- Live proclaimed values
- Guard confidentiality
- Honor deadlines
- Keep appointments
- Do what you say you will do.

When you keep your promises, you show that you are indeed someone who can be counted on to do what you say you will do. In times of uncertainty, people will value your reliability.

44. Remove Doubt

Doubt can be a drag on an organizational change initiative. It cultivates a wait-and-see attitude and can breed cynicism about the change. Do your best to remove doubt.

What do people doubt when it comes to change? Here are some examples:

- Leadership resolve
- The motive for change
- The ability to make the change
- The wisdom of the change itself
- That it's not a passing trend.

Listen for the seeds of doubt in your organization, so you can focus some effort on providing evidence that the doubt is unfounded. For example, if people doubt the ability of the organization to change, demonstrate early successes; if they doubt the motive for change, focus more on proving that the change is important.

45. Laugh About It

When I worked at a strategy execution consulting company, the new CEO (and former medical doctor) addressed the company on a conference call: "I'm a doctor. I've seen people die. What we do here is not that serious." I'm not sure if that was supposed to be a pep talk, but it sent a message: Don't take yourselves too seriously.

Organizational change is not all business and no fun. In fact, if you aren't laughing about it, you're probably doing it wrong! Laughter reduces your own stress, and sharing a laugh with other people in your organization is a great way to show empathy, build relationships and put things in perspective.

So laugh at the absurdity of trying to stop a speeding freight train, or turn the Titanic (or your metaphor of choice). Make fun of your corny acronyms and slogans. Joke about the Weekly Team Progress Status Update meeting. Isn't it funny?

46. Provide Useful Tools

After motivating people with the vision and a sense of urgency, they will understand the What and the Why. They may still be left wondering, How? To that end, provide useful tools to facilitate the change.

Some examples of useful tools to help people change are:
- Meeting facilitation toys and games
- Tracking forms for strategic measures
- Interactive meeting notes
- Forms and templates to complete the job
- Easy-to-find and easy-to-use instructions and flowcharts
- Reminders
- Effective reports.

What defines a useful tool will vary by change initiative. Some people will want to find their own way, so work with them to create something that will work. Others may not have the time to figure it out from scratch, and will be grateful that you didn't leave them to their own devices.

47. Join Forces

Influencing change is not a one-man show. You are not the only person in your organization who feels that change should happen. Whether your initiative is the grassroots variety or the top-down kind, find other people in the organization with the same or similar goals (or complaints) and join forces.

Change is a lot of work. More people means more feet on the ground. Working with others also means that you add strengths that you don't have to your change toolkit. Joining forces with someone in another part of the organization means you can approach the problem from multiple fronts. When you work with others to implement change, you gain more ideas, and you also then have someone to provide you with feedback on your ideas.

Recruit individuals to join you in the inner circle of the change initiative and you will gain ambassadors, partners, and friends.

48. Remove Dead Weight

Let's just be blunt.

If someone is the wrong person for a team, can't contribute appropriately, or hinders the rest of the team's performance, then you might need to ask her to leave the team. If someone can't make (or isn't willing to make) the necessary personal changes and is holding the organization back from achieving its goals, it might be time to remove her from the organization.

This conclusion is harsh, I know. And it should be considered only after addressing her objections and working to get her on board with other influence methods. But hold on to dead weight for too long and the change will drag to a halt.

You might be concerned about the effect on the rest of the team or organization if such a decisive action is taken. Based on my experience, their reaction will probably be relief!

Removing someone who is a roadblock to change sends the message that the organization is serious about change. At the risk of spreading some fear, it may be best to demonstrate your ultimate resolve to stand behind the initiative.

49. Point to the Destination

In their book *Switch: How to Change Things When Change is Hard*, Chip Heath and Dan Heath explain that in order to change, the logical, planning, control-oriented part of our brain needs to know where to go. Similarly, one of John Kotter's eight steps in *Leading Change* is Communicate the Vision. If you want to influence change, point to the destination.

This necessity is best illustrated in the interchange between Alice and the Cheshire Cat in *Alice's Adventures in Wonderland* by Lewis Carroll:

> *One day Alice came to a fork in the road and saw a*
> *Cheshire cat in a tree. "Which road do I take?" she asked.*
> *"Where do you want to go?" was his response.*
> *"I don't know," Alice answered.*
> *"Then," said the cat, "it doesn't matter."*

Communicate the vision. Share what the end result of the change looks like. Point to the destination. That way, people will know in which direction to change.

50. Address Objections

When you introduce a new way of doing things to people in your organization, frequently the first response from them is to come up with all the reasons why it won't work, or why things don't need to change. The criticism can seem harsh, unwarranted, and out of the blue, or... fully expected.

Understand that this response is natural and instinctual. Our brain's automatic response when introduced to a new idea is to reject it as a threat with the fight-or-flight response. It's not a personal affront to you, and it's not a reflection of the change itself. The part of the brain that doesn't think and just reacts responds before the logical part can catch up. That's just the way it works.

My point is – don't respond defensively to people's objections about change. Allow people the opportunity to express their emotional reactions. Acknowledge their concerns and strive to understand them. Then address their objections without making them wrong. Use objections to build the change strategy stronger together.

51. Drop Names

When you are implementing change without having direct authority, sometimes you have to rely on someone else's authority to get things done. One of the easiest ways to borrow someone else's authority is to say (or infer) that you are working on his behalf. In other words, drop names.

The following are examples of name-dropping:
- "The CEO asked me to invite you to participate."
- "Your boss suggested that you would be the one to ask about this."
- "I was at lunch yesterday with the VP of Operations, and she loved this idea."

There are a few warnings about name-dropping. First, make sure the name is worth dropping. If the person whose name you are using isn't respected, or won't back you up, then this tactic may backfire. Also, if you drop names too much, you give the impression that your change initiative can't stand on its own without needing someone to push it through. Plus, you risk becoming someone who can only influence others by relying on other people's authority. It's not a great way to build your own personal influence.

It's probably best to drop names subtly and only occasionally. Drop names to help link your request to the bigger picture, and to connect people with where the change is coming from. Rarely, if ever, should you use it to bulldoze someone.

52. Celebrate Success

In the whirlwind of the day-to-day workplace, often the need to pause and celebrate success is overlooked. Instead, we just keep plugging away at the next thing on the list. To keep the momentum of change going, it is important to take the time to celebrate success.

Change is often a long process. Mark positive milestones, so people feel like there is movement in the right direction. Generating short-term wins and celebrating them reinforces positive movement. It keeps leaders interested and gives them a reason to continue supporting the project. Communicating successes to the rest of the organization bolsters the cause. Acknowledge and reward forward progress so you reinforce what is important and what you want to see more of.

When you are pushing the boulder uphill, it helps to stop long enough to look back and see how far you've gone. Take a celebratory break so you can recoup your energy and realize that you really are making a difference.

53. Connect to Values

In their book *Influencer: The Power to Change Anything*, authors Kerry Patterson et al. write that personal motivation happens by connecting the change to values. They also indicate that one of two questions people ask when deciding whether to try something new is, "Will it be worth it?" (The other is "Can I do it?") Connecting to values motivates change by improving the chance that the answer will be "yes."

The goal is to find a way for individuals to take personal satisfaction from performing the activity or behavior. For example, if team members need to speak up more in meetings, connect the behavior with the value of being open and honest (instead of safety in silence). If you want managers in traditionally competing silos to work together, connect the behavior with the values of community and collaboration (instead of winning). The values and behaviors you select will depend on the initiative, the organization, and the individual's values.

It is also important to make sure the change initiative is aligned with the organization's stated values. Otherwise, one or the other will surely be ignored.

54. Say "Thank You"

Gratitude is an important factor in leading change, especially when you are leading change without authority. After all, no one actually has to do what you say, do they? Luckily, there is an extremely simple and sincere way to express gratitude: Say "thank you."

If someone gives you her time and attention, say "thank you."

If someone tries something new, say "thank you."

If someone tells you why this will never work, say "thank you."

If someone sticks his neck out for you, say "thank you."

If someone shares her opinion or feedback, solicited or not, say "thank you."

If someone lends you his expertise, say "thank you."

If someone invites you to a meeting, say "thank you."

If someone provides an idea, say "thank you."

If someone listens to you, say "thank you."

Organizational change never happens alone. Show appreciation for those who are going on the journey with you, and even those who want to block your path. As a change agent, "Thank you" should be the most common phrase you utter.

55. Be Consistent

When the intent to implement a change is announced, many people want to see proof that it's going to happen. They watch for signs that the change is just a passing fad, that leadership doesn't really mean it. And what are they watching for? Inconsistency.

It's not just the hypocrisy hounds and the skeptics. Everyone to different degrees is aware of conflicting information and purposes. There is so much going on in organizations today that it's easy to find misalignment. Consider the following factors that all need to carry a consistent message during change:

- Vision, mission, values, strategy
- Official communication channels
- Management behavior and conversations with direct reports
- Policies and procedures
- Decisions and priorities
- Goals and measures
- Accountability and incentives
- Training.

Of course, it is impossible to control all these factors on your own. As you roll out the change, place an emphasis on the importance of consistency with those who will carry the message. Become a hypocrisy hound yourself, watching for misalignment so you can address it as it pops up (and it will). In the items you can personally control, evaluate and design them to be consistent.

56. Extend an Invitation

Simply announcing (through an e-mail blast, newsletter, bulletin board, etc.) that an opportunity exists to join in a change project may have limited results. A more effective means of influencing people to participate is a personal invitation.

It's easy for people to dismiss an indiscriminate announcement looking for volunteers. Even someone who is interested in participating may have doubts about whether she is the right person for the project, or may come up with easy excuses for not signing up or taking part in the new activity. On the other hand, if someone is personally invited, you make her feel like she was chosen to take part, and you're recognizing her for her special role in the organization. Plus, it's more difficult to say no to a personal invitation.

Of course, it would be difficult to personally invite every single person in the organization to go through change. The personal invitation is better suited to get the initial people on board, so you can demonstrate to the masses that people are in fact participating. Recruit people up front who have passion for or interest in the change, those who are influential, or those in a visible role... or maybe even someone who might otherwise be your biggest resistor.

57. Find the Emotion

Presentations and meetings about change projects are often filled with numbers, charts, graphs, dollar signs and time lines – a lot of analysis aimed at convincing minds that logically, this is an effort that we should undertake. While quantitative analysis might be the basis for making the decision to change, the motivation for actually changing comes from the heart instead. Find the emotion.

During change, we are moving away from the current state and toward some desired future state. Similarly, there are emotions that repel us and those we would like to experience more of. Here are some examples:

Move Away From	Move Toward
anger	curiosity
annoyance	happiness
anxiety	hope
disgust	love
embarrassment	optimism
fear	pride
frustration	relief
sadness	trust

Remind people often of the negative emotions they are moving away from when they choose to take part in the change. To propel them forward, tap into the positive emotions they will experience.

58. Ask for Help

When it comes to motivation, few things pack as much power as tapping into people's altruistic nature. One way to enlist someone to the cause is simply to ask for his help.

People like to feel needed. When you ask for help, you admit that you can't implement the change on your own, and that the other person holds an important piece of the puzzle. You connect him to a cause greater than himself.

Asking for specific help in small doses works as well. When you request a favor, the understanding is that the person will do it just because it is the nice, friendly thing to do. Often people will take small steps in the right direction just because they want to help the person who asked.

To influence change, appeal to the other person's generosity of spirit, and ask for help.

59. Incite a Riot

Imagine a group of people who are so fed up with the current state of things that they all band together to stand up and do something about it. What if you could harness the energy of a crowd that just decides that enough is enough, we're going to revolt? Perhaps you could even create the circumstances, and incite a riot!

Anger and frustration can be powerful forces that tend to be pent up. Once they get strong enough, they only need a trigger to let loose all that energy. Of course, you don't want to literally incite a riot, with all the chaos and danger that word invokes. But, if you can feed the fire to the point where people say, "We just can't take it anymore!" about the current situation, then your job is to focus all that pent-up frustration into a positive and constructive direction.

Most organizational leaders prefer not to work up their employees into a frenzy, and also like to keep dissatisfaction to a minimum. But if you need to develop a strong sense of urgency to move away from the status quo, inciting a riot might be the way to go.

60. Identify Key Behaviors

I've heard it said that leaders should only point people in the direction they want them to go, and leave them to their own devices to figure out how to get there. In my experience, however, organizational change is usually not just about getting to the end result. Instead, change also entails the way people are accomplishing those results.

Of course, you can't script out every move people should take. You want people to be able to use their creativity and brains to help the organization improve. But, if it matters how people are doing their jobs to accomplish the result, then they should not be left to figure it out for themselves. Let them know the critical few things they need to do.

A few years ago I was involved in an effort to develop a process improvement culture. The concept really didn't sink into the culture until we asked managers to do three things:

1. Ask your direct reports for opportunities for improvement.
2. Have regular work group meetings to develop and implement solutions.
3. Keep track and report back the status of their ideas to the group.

Until we incorporated the behaviors into the fabric of the department manager's job and relationship with their team, the process improvement concept was just a side project. Identify the key behaviors that people should incorporate into their jobs and see change get embedded into how things are done.

61. Keep It Simple

While running a 2-year training program in advanced Balanced Scorecard concepts, I had the privilege of working with a number of strategy management professionals, all of whom were leading large-scale changes from the middle of their organizations. Most had a similar issue: their organizations' scorecards had too many objectives and measures (Kaplan and Norton recommend no more than 25).

Although they knew they should narrow down the strategy to the critical few, the scorecards ballooned because either their executive teams tried to be all things to all people, or because no one wanted their department to be left out of the organization's strategy. The result? Extra effort, reduced focus, and added complexity.

With the uncertainty already inherent in change, the last thing you want to do is add confusion. Overload leads to glazed looks and dug-in heels. You've got to try to keep it simple.

Where does complexity appear? Here are just a few of the places to look:

- Goals, objectives, measures
- Processes
- Communication
- Policies
- Incentives.

When in doubt, choose simple.

62. Share What Works

The road to change is rife with obstacles and underlying issues that can seem overwhelming when you think of trying to fix it all. The authors of *Switch: How to Change Things When Change is Hard* suggest that instead of trying to solve all the organization's problems, find areas of the organization that work well, and then share their techniques with the rest of the organization.

We already have fancy names for this: "internal benchmarking" and "best practice sharing." These sound very bureaucratic, don't they? You don't need to institutionalize it. Just find the people who are already doing what you want everyone else to do, and let them tell, show and share what they do that works.

- Which departments have effective meetings that are fun to go to? Invite other people so they can see how that team interacts.
- Who has added a special tweak to their process that improves overall quality? Provide them time to show others what they do differently.
- Who has created a unique tool that allows them to complete the job in half the time? Help them develop instructions and duplicate it for others.
- Which managers' teams are achieving their goals? Watch how they encourage their direct reports and hold them accountable.

Identify the parts of your organization that are already working the new way, and shine a light on them.

63. Adjust the Environment

I once worked in a building where the official name of the wall color was Touch of Gray. It was stark raving neutral with a hint of depression! I spiced it up by hanging colorful curtains and reupholstering the gray cubicle walls that made up my desk with red fabric. Suddenly my office became a wellspring of ideas and a place that I wanted to sit and work.

Our physical environment affects our perceptions and emotions, and enables our activities. It's best if the environment in your organization aligns with the change you want to implement. Ask yourself:

- Are conference rooms equipped and decorated in ways that support how you want people to act in meetings?
- Do the layouts of break rooms and other gathering locations facilitate the types of interactions you want to create?
- Does the flow of the manufacturing floor or the distribution area enable good decisions?
- Do the plaques and displays in the lobby give the right impression about the direction the organization is going and the things you want to celebrate?
- What adjustments might you make to the parking lot? The mail room?

We are very much connected to the world in which we live and work. Take an inventory of the environment of your organization, and see what might be adjusted to help support your change.

64. Hold Them Accountable

Change often requires that a number of people agree to take on tasks that they will perform on their own. The odds are reduced that people will follow through on their commitments if they believe no one will follow up and make sure that they did it. To influence change, hold people accountable.

Keep track of the things people say they will do, and check in to see if they have completed them. Give them a forum to report their progress. Help people stay on task and on time. Discuss how they can effectively be held accountable, and define what that means. Make sure to agree on the consequences if they don't maintain their part of the project.

When someone doesn't follow through, explore what happened that prevented her from success; not to find fault, but to better understand what is holding her back. Then help her find what she needs to succeed. If there were defined consequences, always follow through.

Accountability can be a 4-letter word in organizations where it is misunderstood as punishment. Define what it means in your organization in the spirit of helping people do what they say they will do.

65. Induce Guilt

As behavior modification goes, guilt and its partner shame are effective – albeit demoralizing – tactics for getting people to fall in line. The feeling of guilt is caused by making someone believe he has done something wrong and that he should blame himself for it. The bad experience is the impetus for that person to conform to the "right" way next time.

Any behavior we use to convey judgment of someone else has the potential to induce guilt. A stern reprimand, a disgusted eye roll, an incredulous look, a snicker. The key is to make the person feel bad for stepping out of the norm, going against group values, breaking the rules, or doing something wrong.

People generally don't want to be around others who make them feel guilty all the time, so I don't recommend this as a long-term influence strategy. However, we all induce guilt from time to time without necessarily thinking about it, mainly because it tends to work in small doses.

66. Respect Resistance

Anyone who tries to implement change in an organization experiences resistance. While it shows up as overt challenges or complaints, it also appears as a more subtle digging-in of heels. Missed deadlines. Rescheduled meetings. Sticking with the usual. Hesitance. Silence.

The experience of resistance for change agents is personal. A recent post on Twitter said it best, "Resistance = Other people are not doing things I want them to do [with] the speed or enthusiasm that I desire." I liken the feeling to pushing a boulder uphill. It's easy to get frustrated when it seems like people are not listening to you.

Resistance is not something that can be overcome or pushed aside. The harder you push, the harder you will be pushed against. If you were able to bulldoze through resistance, you will have reached the other side without bringing anyone else along. Instead, respect resistance.

Resistance itself is not bad. In fact, it is perfectly normal and justified. Humans like things to stay the same, be predictable, remain safe. It's written in our brains to either fight or run away from things that we perceive as threats to our security.

Approach resistance with curiosity. Resistance serves as an opportunity to improve the change process. It helps you clarify what to do next. Sometimes it gives a warning of something about to go wrong. When you seek to understand resistance, you give people an opportunity to be heard. Work with resistance instead of against it.

67. Go First

Every organizational change initiative needs a leader. (Actually, lots of leaders.) When we think of a leader, generally we think of someone who creates a vision, influences people to get on board, and holds people accountable to staying on track. But practically speaking, a leader is the one who is first in line, whom everyone else is following. Someone needs to go first.

People do not follow someone who says, "Go *that* way." Instead, a leader says, "Come *this* way." You can't expect someone else to test the waters. A leader needs to step forward, to try it out, and show that it's going to be okay – or at least that the people who follow will not be alone.

Even as you lead change from the middle, you have the opportunity to go first. You can step forward and demonstrate to people at your own level in the organization that it is safe to speak up and take action to make a difference. Anything you create to help people change the way they work, you must be willing to try first. Also, use your own influence with organizational leaders to help them go first.

68. Gain Commitment

When discussing organizational change, we often talk about the necessity of gaining buy-in for the initiative. In poker, buy-in is the minimum bet required to play the game. Similarly, buy-in of change is simply agreement that the project should go forward. To gain momentum, you really need people to go beyond buy-in. Instead, gain commitment.

Commitment means people pledge to do their part to implement change. It is much more than simply head-nodding. Those who are committed to change complete tasks, strive to achieve goals and align their words with their actions.

In *Influence: The Psychology of Persuasion*, the author shows that if people commit, orally or in writing, to an idea or goal, then they are more likely to honor that commitment. The desire to not contradict oneself is so strong that, even if the original incentive or motivation is removed after someone has already agreed, she will likely continue to honor the agreement.

So, make sure people are writing down or saying out loud that they will implement change. For more powerful commitment, get them to be as specific as possible about what they will say and do to support the change.

69. Make It Fun

It is easy to think that in order for people to take your initiative seriously, you have to be, well, serious. My general observation about life is that most people are happier, more open minded, and less defensive when they are having fun than when they are being serious. If people are smiling while participating in the change, it means they are enjoying it and will want to continue the experience! Why not make it fun?

Play and humor help with many aspects of change. Here are some of the things you can accomplish by adding fun:

- Gain attention
- Kick people out of their comfort zones
- Neutralize office politics
- Entice people to participate
- Make it memorable
- Increase creativity.

You don't have to be serious for people to take the change seriously. Fun will reinforce the change when it is consistent and aligned with other messages. So add humor. Incorporate play. Include a game. Be silly. Make it fun!

70. Be Flexible

The path of change is not linear. Nor is it predictable. Circumstances change. The urgent pops up and pushes attention aside. People react to change in ways you don't expect. Others say one thing and do the opposite. The new system you designed doesn't work the way it should. It costs more than you thought. All kinds of things occur that throw you off your original plan.

As a change agent, it can be tempting to stick to your plan about how change should happen. But when something new and unexpected happens, you suddenly have a new reality that is different from the one you started with. You will have to readjust your approach in order to continue forward.

Be flexible. Keep an open mind about alternate routes to the same end result. Don't bang your head against the wall trying to stick to the way you thought it should work. If what you're trying isn't working, try something else. Dance with it.

After all, how compelling is a change agent who can't change himself?

71. Measure Progress

If you got all the way to the end of your change initiative and then finally looked to see if you made it to the intended destination, you would probably be disappointed. Although truthfully, you probably would never make it to the end, because everyone would have given up on the project a long time ago without any evidence of improvement.

As a project manager, measure progress so you can see if what you are doing is working. That way, you can make adjustments as you go to help keep your initiative on track.

As a change agent, measure progress so you can help people see that their efforts are paying off. In the middle of a long change initiative, it might feel like nothing is happening despite a lot of work. It will help to have a way to say, "Look how far we've come!"

How often should you measure progress? Every year, quarter, month, week, day...? The answer depends on what you are measuring. You don't want the time between measurements to be so short that you won't see progress in between because nothing moved. But, you also don't want to wait so long that you'll find out too late that you should have made an adjustment sooner. Find a frequency that will show concrete progress and also provide timely information for making decisions.

72. Be Patient

Fact: we can't change the attitudes and habits of others. We can only do our best to influence, and let them take care of changing themselves. And that happens in other people's timing, not necessarily in yours. Sometimes, the best thing you can do is just stand back and wait.

Introduce an idea, and give people time to warm up to it. Implement a new system or process, and let people figure out for themselves that it will work. Forge a new path, and allow people a chance to catch up.

Organizational change is not an immediate phenomenon. Thankfully so – if things changed as quickly as we wished they would, we would all have whiplash! So be patient, and know that you can use all the influence strategies you want, but you can't bypass the change itself.

73. Shrink It

Large change initiatives can seem huge and daunting. A grand vision may be good for inspiration, but it can also freeze people with that deer-in-headlights feeling. It helps to narrow down a large change, which might seem impossible, into practical steps. Shrink the change, so it becomes manageable.

Whether your organization is implementing a new strategy, installing a large-scale program, or completing a merger, individuals can feel disconnected from the change. Beyond asking, "What's in it for me," people will not know how to act until they know how they fit into the puzzle.

Break down the initiative into doable chunks. Set short-term targets. Identify the critical behaviors that people should perform. Show how each department or process has a unique part in the change. Link individual activities to the larger project. Split the initiative into smaller projects. Shrink the change into something people believe they can accomplish.

74. Establish Authority

If you don't have direct authority as a manager or leader in your organization, you can gain authority in other ways. Your personal influence as a change agent relies on your ability to build up and utilize your expert power. To influence change, establish authority.

Having authority allows you to do many things to help implement change, such as:

- Take action without permission
- Make decisions that affect other people
- Model behavior
- Change minds
- Provide feedback.

In the short term, you can establish authority by speaking up and demonstrating the skills and knowledge you already have. Share your observations, and be assertive when you see something that will throw the change off track. In the long run, support your role as change agent by continually increasing your knowledge – in your choice of professions as well as in organizational change.

75. Get Leadership Support

As a change agent, you know what it is like to try to be responsible for implementing an initiative without really having the authority to get it done. Since you are trying to influence change without authority, you need to partner with others who have authority to help move things along. Eventually, you need to get leadership support.

Beyond buy-in, leadership support for change means they are committed to the implementation. Their actions match their words. They hold people accountable. They make decisions that are consistent with the change. They communicate frequently. They back you up as change agent. In a nutshell, it means they are doing what needs to be done to implement change – and not doing things that contradict or obstruct it.

Getting leadership support is a common struggle for those who are implementing change from the middle of an organization. My *Beyond Buy-in* Workbook provides five steps to gain support. They include: determining whose support you need, defining what support really means, and figuring out how to get that support.

Leaders must understand the importance of their role in change and also agree to accept that role. Without leadership support, the scope of your change relies on your own personal span of influence. With disinterested leaders, it is only a matter of time before your initiative halts or fizzles away.

76. Recognize Success

When you are busy fighting fires, or shoring up dams, or generally focused on what's next, it is easy to forget to stop and see what has already gone right. By continually looking at what is not working yet, you can make it seem like you are spinning your wheels. To keep up your own energy and to keep from demoralizing the rest of the organization, it is important to stop and acknowledge how far you have come.

Recognizing success requires first that you know what success looks like. Success means achieving goals, performing desired behaviors, and reaching milestones. Sometimes, it can be more subtle, like movement in the right direction, or changing minds one at a time. Look ahead and decide what success means at each step.

Next, you must be able to see that you and others have attained some success. On a regular basis, step back from the constant push forward to take stock of the distance covered. Search for and acknowledge the positive effects that have occurred as a result of the change initiative.

Then, let people know about it. Remind people what they have accomplished so far. Thank them for their efforts. Reinforce the progress to date by recognizing and communicating success when it happens.

77. Generate Short-Term Wins

Straight out of John Kotter's playbook, *Leading Change*, it is important for the success of a long-term initiative to generate short-term wins. These are milestones that are set in the near future, which are deliberately chosen to demonstrate early success.

Short-term wins help build momentum by proving that the initiative will actually work. Demonstrating early success can help get the naysayers and holdouts on board.

When selecting the short-term milestone or project, choose wisely. If possible, you want to pick a project that has all three of the following qualities:

- It is important.
- It has a high likelihood of success.
- It can achieve success within the attention span of those who want an excuse to write the initiative off (usually a few months).

A project that has all three qualities may be elusive. Usually, if something is too easy or short-term, it's probably not that important (or else it would have been done already). If you can, come up with a milestone that is sufficiently important and short-term. Then, invest your time and effort into making sure it happens!

Once you complete the first wins, you will want to continually produce short-term wins to keep the momentum going, and keep the attention of those who need proof that the initiative is making progress.

78. Eliminate Noise

We live in a noisy world. Distractions abound. In the workplace, your initiative can be easily drowned out amongst everything else going on that keeps the place running. Not to mention the non-work-related stuff that people fill their attention with the rest of the time.

Give people the opportunity to hear what they actually need to hear, so they can do what needs to be done. Find ways to eliminate noise.

First, eliminate noise in the environment where the change occurs. During meetings or training when you want to keep the focus on the task at hand, close the door. Put up a "Do not disturb" sign. Turn off the office phone ringer. Put the mobile on vibrate. Turn off e-mail notifications. Put away any other workplace distractions that add to the noise.

Then, look at the noise produced by the initiative itself. There is so much information whizzing by, and everything that people don't need to read, watch or hear is noise. Target your message so the people who need to hear it do, and those who don't need to hear it aren't bothered by it. Monitor the other competing messages that are produced by the organization. Can some be put on hold so there is more focus on the initiative? Eliminate all the extra stuff that, bit by bit, hogs the attention span of your audience.

79. Flatter

The saying goes, "Flattery will get you nowhere," but anyone who has been given a well-placed compliment knows it can go a long way. Make someone feel good about himself, and he is likely to reciprocate by helping you, doing what you ask, or otherwise opening himself up to influence.

Of course, someone will see through an over-the-top compliment given just before a request is made. He will know you are buttering him up. One of my coaching clients was so effusive with flattery that people stopped believing almost everything he said, and it became an integrity issue. Avoid saying things that aren't true or that are exaggerated.

If you can brighten someone's day with a genuine acknowledgment, he is bound to repay it. Watch for opportunities to give someone a compliment, and increase your ability to influence change.

80. Empower

According to *Influencer: The Power to Change Anything*, there are two things people need in order to change – motivation and ability. The ability to change includes having the authority within the organization to do so. Empower employees so they are able to make the required changes on their own.

People going through change need the freedom to take action and try new behaviors. They must have some authority to make decisions and do things their own way. If you want people to ultimately own and embody the change, it needs to be their choice.

Managers often stand in the way of the very change they say they want, because they don't really empower their people. Instead, they micromanage, nitpick, say "no," and otherwise discourage their employees by not really letting them change. Maintaining too much control may result in malicious compliance; you will end up getting only what you ask for, instead of what you really want.

81. Nag

Wouldn't it be nice if people would just do what you need the first time you ask? Alas, sometimes people drag their feet. Others continue to do the same old behavior, or forget to do a new one. In those instances, a few repetitive requests or reminders might do the trick. That's right, it's time to nag!

The art of nagging requires annoying someone into submission. It means persistently reminding someone until the person gets fed up and does what you need. If someone asks, "What are you, my *Mother*?" then you are on the right track!

The risk of nagging is that you might get a reputation for being annoying. He might dig in his heels further. If you have already made a request 5 times, there is a high likelihood that there is some other form of resistance in play than forgetfulness or procrastination. Before the nagging gets to that level, ask what might be holding him back, and offer to help.

82. Enlist Early Adopters

Like the adoption rate of new technology, people getting on board with change follow a typical bell curve. Leading the way, there are the innovators – the people like you, who are implementing the change. Then, a few early adopters come on. Next, the majority sees that the early adopters are having success, so they jump on. Last are the laggards, who eventually – or never – decide to accept the inevitable.

One of your jobs as the change agent is to facilitate the first people to participate. Until you do, no one else will be coming with you! To kick-start the process, enlist early adopters.

Different people will be early adopters depending on your project. But there are three categories of people who will typically sign up to help first:

- Those who believe in what you are doing and want to be a part of it.
- Friends who believe in you personally, want to help you succeed, and think you are capable of delivering.
- People who would like nothing better than to have an excuse to get out of their cubicle.

By definition, early adopters for your change are fairly easy to convince to get on board. All you have to do is find them, ask, and help them remove any obstacles that would prevent them from participating.

83. Increase Awareness

I've heard it said that awareness is the first step toward change. Before you can change anything, you have to see that something exists that needs improvement. To influence change, increase awareness.

Some of the things that should be brought to light are:
- Culture and its effect on behavior – and the behaviors that maintain the culture
- Processes that people use to really get things done
- Undiscussables, 400 lb gorillas, and other remnants of fear
- Consequences of not changing.

Be bold. Shine a light in the shadows of the organization. Point out the things that hide in plain sight. Make people aware of the everyday forces that hold the organization on its current trajectory. Give people a heavy dose of reality. Only when you increase awareness can change start to occur.

84. Install New Habits

Most organizational change consists of breaking old habits and creating new ones. The status quo, after all, is just doing what you're used to doing, on autopilot. One role of the change agent is to install new habits.

Habits are the activities and behaviors that require no planning or intentional thought processes for them to occur. They are likely to be hiding in plain sight. Look for existing habits in the following areas:

- Forms and processes
- Meeting rituals
- Knee-jerk reactions
- Routine activities.

By the end of your change initiative, you want the new way to be automatic; in fact, the initiative is not fully complete until that happens. Break old habits by adding reminders and removing enabling artifacts. Install new habits through practice and repetition until the new way feels natural again.

85. Threaten

I recently had a conversation with a plant manager about a quality initiative his team was implementing. He talked about all the training they were doing for plant employees. I said, "Yes, but what is their motivation to learn it?" He replied, "*Or else.*" In other words, learn this and use it correctly, *or else* you won't work here any more.

Some people just won't change until you light a fire under them. As a last resort, it might help to inform someone that if he doesn't play along, something bad is going to happen to him. To get someone to change, sometimes you have to threaten him!

The manner in which you send this message makes all the difference, since you don't want to crank up the fear factor to paralyzing levels. It's more effective in the long term if it sounds like a kind warning instead of intimidation. If your next course of action is to get his boss involved, it might be a good idea to bring this up, so he has the opportunity to act before that happens.

Of course, I would never condone or recommend the use of physical violence or verbal abuse. The threats I'm talking about are ethical consequences or punishments that you have the authority to carry out within the normal bounds of acceptable organizational behavior.

86. Assign Responsibility

Change doesn't spontaneously happen on its own. If you want something to change, it must have someone's name attached. The people who must take on the change, or incorporate it into their job, must know that it is theirs to do so. To make change personal, assign responsibility.

The first reason to assign responsibility is to make sure it gets done. Give people responsibility for tasks and decisions. Put their initials in the meeting minutes next to the things they need to do. Also, encourage people to take responsibility for their own responses, behaviors, and attitudes regarding the change.

Another purpose of assigning responsibility is to pass on ownership of the project. When people are responsible for a piece of the change, they feel more in control of their change experience. And more control means less resistance to the change itself. Let people know that the change is not happening to them, and it is a positive result of their own efforts.

Last, you can't do everything yourself to implement the change. Delegate, and allow people the authority to get things done and move the project forward.

87. Build Relationships

Your ability to personally influence someone depends on your relationship with her. If you don't know her at all, you will have minimal, if any influence. If she knows your name and face, she might pay some attention. But if you have a relationship with her, there is a better chance that she will listen, care, and take action based on what you say. To increase your personal influence, build relationships.

It's just a fact that you have more influence with people who like you and trust you. Take a look at the relationships you have with people who have a big impact on your change initiative. When you see them in the hall, do you make eye contact? Do you say hello? Do you stop and talk? The nature of the relationship will also affect how you might influence someone. Is your relationship built on respect, authority, and expertise, or on humor, service and friendship?

By building a relationship, you find out what makes the other person tick. You can better understand her concerns, her trigger points, and what she cares about. You can learn what she needs most from the change, and how you might support her through it. Likewise, she can get to know you, and understand what you are trying to do and why it is important to you.

88. Share in the Design

Often, when we think of change management, we think of top-down driven initiatives. Someone decides where to take the organization, or what system to install, and then the task is to implement the idea. However, there is another route that is less heavy-handed. You identify and lead people to see the need for change, but then the details for how the organization will change is more of a collaborative effort. Instead of the final vision being sent down from on high, many other layers can share in the design of the change itself.

Before the path is deemed, involve people in the design. On a small scale, let the users help select new software, or enlist people to select the method for redesigning processes. For more organization-wide projects, use large group methods, like World Cafe or Open Space Technology, to build the collective direction for the organization. When you find yourself making a decision that impacts how the change will happen, ask yourself whether it is possible to include others in the decision.

When you share in the design, you provide not just a sense of ownership, but actual ownership! The participants help bring the path to life. They can see their contribution. And they have more of a stake in seeing it happen.

89. Reduce Risk

The hesitation to change behaviors or participate in new activities is often caused by fear. Fear is the emotion attached to a perceived risk. It's the worry that if one thing happens, then something bad will follow as a result. To negate fear, reduce risk.

Fear comes in all shapes and sizes, but when it comes to change, there are some common ones. Fear of being wrong. Fear of looking dumb. Fear that I'm not able. Fear of extra work. Fear of losing control or power. People who resist change believe that there is a risk that the fear will be realized if they participate, so they dig in their heels, sometimes without knowing it.

As an emotion, fear is not always rational. By surfacing the underlying risk assumption, you can take practical steps to alleviate it. For example, if you see that someone believes she will not be able to perform a task adequately, how might you reduce the risk that she will be unsuccessful when she tries? You might also reduce the perceived risk by raising awareness of the real likelihood of failure.

90. Establish Deadlines

Tasks that are left open-ended have a tendency to be postponed indefinitely, especially when people are busy doing other things. Without a due date, activities that are easier, more fun, or more urgent might take precedence over those required to implement your project. Establish deadlines to let people know when things need to be done.

Setting deadlines helps people better plan their work. It aligns people with others who are waiting for the job to be done. And, it gives those who tend to be deadline-driven a reason to get started.

People may still miss deadlines because they forget, or it's not a priority, or they procrastinate. Set reminders. Communicate a sense of urgency. Seek to understand any underlying resistance to getting tasks done on time. Help people meet their deadlines once they are set.

91. Foster Resilience

Resilience is the ability to bounce back after change. It is the speed with which things return to normal after a disruption. The more resilient people are in your organization, the better they are able to incorporate changes into their work without experiencing more stress than they can handle. Especially in times of constant change, foster resilience.

There are multiple facets of resilience that you can help people with:
- Mental: Focus on positive thoughts instead of negative ones, control perspectives
- Emotional: Manage emotional reactions to the change
- Physical: Give people the opportunity to relax so they don't get exhausted from the project
- Social: Readjust to the new social structure, negotiate relationships, develop support systems.

Without resilience, people may check out, jump ship, or just be running at lower capacity because they can't get their footing back. As a change agent, your job is not complete until people feel like they are back to normal again – a new normal that incorporates all the changes they have undergone. Help people learn to bounce back.

92. Set Clear Goals

A change initiative must have clear goals in order to succeed –
otherwise, how would you know if you have actually succeeded? Goals
serve several purposes: They provide direction and alignment, so
people know collectively what they are aiming for. They build
motivation by offering a challenge to strive for. Plus, goals are a means
of ensuring accountability.

A clear goal consists of 5 distinct parts:
- Objective: Describe, in words, what the goal of the initiative is.
- Measure: Identify what you will track to assess progress.
- Target: Determine what measure value you are aiming for.
- Due date: Select the date by when you want to reach the target.
- Responsibility: Assign whose job it is to accomplish the goal.

The Balanced Scorecard methodology offers a good framework for goal-
setting. It offers four categories of objectives that you might consider
for your project. Financial objectives measure the dollars, of course.
Customer objectives determine success from the customer point of view
(including internal customers). Internal Process goals show the
mechanics of how you will achieve the initiative. In the last group are
Organizational Capacity objectives, which detail how the organization
will support the initiative. Making sure you have goals in each of these
areas gives you a complete look at what you are trying to accomplish.

93. Entertain

If you are an organizational change agent, think of yourself as the host of the change. Like the host of an event, it's your role to decide whom to invite. To keep track of who plans to attend. To welcome people and take care of the items they bring with them. To ensure their comfort and keep them well fed. To provide relevant activities and to introduce the right people to each other. To monitor that it doesn't get too loud or rowdy. And to clean up afterward. In a nutshell, it's your job to entertain!

The host also creates the atmosphere for the event. Is your project a comedy, a mystery, a drama, a thriller? What is the theme for your initiative? When you entertain, you craft the experience that will help people understand and move through the change while giving them a reason to pay attention and participate.

94. Incorporate into Identity

When the change is truly accomplished, a necessary caveat is that the person who has gone through the change has in some way incorporated it into their identity. That is, they see the new attitude, behavior or activity as who they are and what they do.

For example, if your initiative includes increasing creative ideas from employees, then one requirement is to help those employees see that they are, in fact, creative. Instead of thinking of all the ways to enable people to act creatively, or motivate them to be creative, you could help each person think of himself as someone who is already creative.

No matter how effectively you motivate and encourage someone, if he believes he is not someone who would or could participate in the change, then you are stuck in an uphill battle. But, if you can change his perspective and give him a new identity, you can eliminate a lot of struggle and resistance. Once you make the change a part of who he is, your job is simply to help get obstacles out of his way.

95. Design Choices

According to the authors of *Nudge: Improving Decisions about Health, Wealth, and Happiness*, actively selecting the "choice architecture" can influence the decision that is made. In other words, you can present options in such a way that encourages certain choices and discourages others.

Some of the design factors you might consider are:
- Location: Place the choice you want people to select in the most readily available or visible spot.
- Number of choices: Keep the number of choices small, so people don't become overwhelmed and give up.
- Limited choices: Limit the options to the ones you want people to select from. When I offer my kids breakfast, I give them the choice of Cheerios or Rice Krispies – not Cheerios or cookies!
- Relative choices: Since people compare between the options they are given, offer choices that are not as desirable compared to the one you want them to make.
- Default: Make the default option the one you want people to select.

People generally want the freedom to make their own decisions. When they make their own decisions, they feel more ownership and commitment toward the choice they make. As a change agent, you can guide those decisions by designing their choices.

96. Show Respect

I have never known anyone who can implement sustainable change without showing respect to the people going through the change. I firmly believe that genuine respect for others is the foundation for being an effective change agent. Change happens when individuals, each with her own sense of pride and dignity, decide that it is worth it to change. If you don't respect each person for who she is and what she brings to the organization, you come off as arrogant. Show respect and put people at the center of your change strategy.

Respect starts with your belief that each person going through the change is on equal footing with you as a human being. That her participation matters. That she is individually worth the investment in time and money. And that she is capable of making the change.

Treat people like they want to be treated. Involve people, not as a necessary evil, but because the organization will be better for their participation. When you encounter inevitable resistance, attribute it not to their being difficult, but to reasonable reactions to the forces of change. Every person has the potential to make a contribution. Treat them all as if they matter – because they do!

97. Harness Peer Pressure

The urge to conform to a group norm is powerful. When implementing change, this force can work against you, since no one wants to step out and break the existing unspoken rules. When you harness peer pressure, it can be used to get people to work by a new set of norms as well.

One way to harness peer pressure is to be very deliberate and open about it. Within a group, explicitly agree on the new way of acting, and commit to a group response when someone strays from the new way. Encourage members of the group to hold each other accountable.

As a facilitator, you can use it more subtly. For example, if you have a couple of members of a team that are not completing their tasks on time, start the meeting with updates from those who have completed theirs first. It will be more evident to the slackers that everyone else is performing their part.

Similarly, you can introduce a new person to an existing group that has already adopted a new behavior. The group will indoctrinate the new person naturally. Once they are done, you can rotate in someone else until everyone is on board with the program.

98. Communicate

No change initiative can occur successfully without proper internal communication. Convey messages to audiences to keep people informed and mobilize the organization for change. Communication is a means to gain attention, educate, and get individuals and groups to take action to move the change initiative forward.

When it comes to communication about change, I often hear things like "You can't over-communicate!" or "Communicate seven times, seven different ways!" It seems like you should unleash a tidal wave of information at people. Instead, create a focused collection of messages that tell a compelling story of change. You need a communication plan that:

- Gets the appropriate message to the right person so they do something with it
- Ensures consistency between media and messengers
- Overcomes the rapidly increasing amount of information that distracts employees from your message
- Communicates enough, in quantity and content, to impart the message effectively.

We often think of internal communication as official items like newsletters, intranet, videos, or all-hands meetings. But, it also includes more informal meetings and conversations. The most influential internal communication source is the immediate boss of each person.

99. Offer Incentives

Incentives are a source of extrinsic motivation – meaning the source of the motivation is coming from outside an individual. If you achieve a goal or perform at a certain level, then you will get something extra besides your pride and self-satisfaction. Offer incentives to reinforce the motivation to change.

Some of the types of incentives you might offer are:
- Money: Cash, gift cards, bonuses
- Merchandise: Clothing, trinkets, other physical items
- Events: Parties, ceremonies, travel
- Awards: Certificates, plaques

Because the psychology of motivation can be tricky, incentives often have unintended consequences. Make sure your incentive is in sync with the result or behavior you want to motivate. Avoid creating awards that conflict with stated values or goals. And remember, not everyone is motivated by the same thing.

Additional Resources

The following is the original list of books from which I drew inspiration. Specific references are included in the text of this book. For more detail, I recommend reading these books.

Co-Active Coaching, Laura Whitworth et al., Davies-Black Publishing, Second Edition 2007.

Driving Fear Out of The Workplace, Kathleen Ryan and Daniel Oestreich, Jossey-Bass, 1998.

Influencer, The Power to Change Anything, Kerry Patterson et al., McGraw-Hill, 2007.

Influence: The Psychology of Persuasion, Robert Cialdini, Harper Paperbacks, Revised Edition 2006.

Leading Change, John Kotter, Harvard Business Press, 1996.

Managing at the Speed of Change, Daryl Conner, Random House, 1993.

Nudge, Improving Decisions about Health, Wealth, and Happiness Richard Thaler and Cass Sunstein, Penguin, 2009.

Predictably Irrational, Dan Ariely, Harper Perennial, Revised Edition 2010.

Switch: How to Change Things When Change is Hard, Chip Heath and Dan Heath, Crown Business, 2010.

The Transparency Edge: How Credibility Can Make or Break You in Business, Elizabeth Pagano and Barbara Pagano, McGraw-Hill, 2005.

The *Beyond Buy-in* Workbook walks you through five straight-forward steps to figure out how to gain the most important ingredient for change success: the support of leadership. More than just how to get to "yes," *Beyond Buy-in* answers the question, "How do I get leaders to do what they need to do to drive the change forward?"

The *Pinpoint Communication* Kit, which includes customizable PowerPoint templates, provides a practical step-by-step process for creating a communication plan for your change initiative. *Pinpoint Communication* answers the question, "How do I get the appropriate message to the right people?"

The *Change Starts Here* Workbook guides you through four steps to clarify your change initiative. *Change Starts Here* answers the question, "What am I really trying to change, and how am I going to do it?"

The *Change Starts Here* workbook is available free with your newsletter subscription.

www.enclaria.com/publications

About the Author

As founder of Enclaria LLC, Heather Stagl equips individuals to push the boulder uphill at work. She provides a number of resources for organizational change practitioners, including individual coaching, training programs and step-by-step workbooks. Heather is a blogger and radio host of "The Change Agent's Dilemma: How to Influence Change Without Authority" on BlogTalkRadio.

For more than a decade, Heather has implemented a wide variety of strategic initiatives as an internal change agent, including IT systems, a process improvement program, and strategy execution with the Balanced Scorecard. She was the Director of Organizational Effectiveness at a mid-size food manufacturer headquartered in the Chicago suburbs. After moving to Atlanta, she conducted a two-year working group program on strategy execution at Balanced Scorecard Collaborative. She holds a Bachelor of Science in Industrial Engineering from Northwestern University and an MBA in Leadership and Change Management from DePaul University. Heather completed coach training at The Coaches Training Institute.

Heather currently resides north of Atlanta with her husband and two young children.

www.enclaria.com

Made in the USA
San Bernardino, CA
09 January 2013